AF488036

Hooligans, Rebels, and Rabble-Rousers

Hooligans, Rebels, and Rabble-Rousers

Written & Illustrated by
Paula Kerman

atmosphere press

© 2024 Paula Kerman

Published by Atmosphere Press

Artwork by Paula Kerman

Cover design by Matthew Fielder

No part of this book may be reproduced without permission from the author except in brief quotations and in reviews.

Atmospherepress.com

For girls of all ages
who dare to
speak their truth and
make their voices heard.

Table of Contents

Introduction

This book tells the true stories of twenty girls who did not have perfect lives.

But all of them had one thing in common: COURAGE.

What they did was often not popular. Ruth Bader Ginsburg was repeatedly told by men that she did not belong because she was a woman. But Ruth was a feminist, which means that she believed that men and women are equal, which they obviously are! Naomi Osaka was criticized for refusing to do a news conference after an important tennis match. She believed that it was hard on the mental health of the tennis players.

What they did was often dangerous. When Malala spoke out publicly on the importance of education for girls, she was shot by the Taliban, who would not allow girls to go to school. Lozen, an Apache woman, fought bravely against the invading military that was trying to take away her tribe's land.

What they did was creative. Aretha Franklin used her powerful singing voice to inspire. Her song "Respect" was an anthem or hymn for the civil rights movement and the Women's Movement. Frida Kahlo was an artist who suffered a lot of pain after a terrible accident. She painted her reality and "turned her pain into beauty."

I wrote and illustrated this book because I experienced many losses in a short time. I needed to be strong to get through this, and these women inspired me.

As a mother, teacher, and artist, I wanted to create a book that tells the stories of what these feisty women were like as children, and how they overcame tough times to become amazing and courageous women. I want my readers to know they are not alone. Each of us has the ability to rise above and make positive changes. Each of us can be a part of this tribe of hooligans, rebels, and rabble-rousers in our own way.

There's a saying: "Well-behaved women rarely make history." Go out and use your voice to make the world a better place!

Lozen

Apache Warrior and Healer

Born 1840 in Apacheria, New Mexico
Died 1889 in Mount Vernon, Alabama

Lozen was born in an area called Apacheria, which was Arizona, New Mexico, and part of Mexico. Later, it was called New Mexico. She spent most of her time with her older brother, Victorio, who was an important Apache chief. She learned to ride a horse at age seven.

It was a brutal time for the Apaches with enemies on all sides. Mexico was paying for Apache scalps, and the Americans were trying to take their land and food and kill their people.

Lozen showed many abilities that were unusual for her age. While other girls were in charge of the home and community, Lozen learned how to use a spear, bow, and rifle. She was determined to help her people.

She also exhibited special powers. At her coming-of-age ceremony, around age twelve, Lozen saw a vision of herself as a healer or medicine woman. She studied herbs and minerals and used them to heal wounds. She also discovered a special power to predict where the enemy was coming from. She got up at sunrise, face to the sun. She turned in circles with her arms held out until her hands tingled. Her palms would turn purple if the enemy was approaching.

She was a valuable help to her tribe because of this. She helped them avoid capture in this way and became a legend among her people.

Many men of the tribe wanted to marry her, but Lozen was not interested. She was too busy! When soldiers were after her people, she led women and children across a raging Rio Grande to safety. Once they were safe on the other side, she rode back across the river to continue fighting the enemy. "She could ride, shoot, and fight like a man," her brother said. "Lozen is my right hand."

Lozen escorted a woman and her newborn across the desert of Mexico. She had only a rifle, cartridge belt, knife, and a three-day supply of food. Through raining gunfire, she delivered them to the reservation.

After her brother Victorio was killed in battle, Lozen joined forces with the famous Apache war chief Geronimo. They tried to negotiate a peace treaty. The Americans did not take them seriously. Finally, the Apaches laid down their weapons and surrendered. Geronimo, Lozen, and others were sent by train to a swampy prisoner camp in Florida. She was later transferred to another prison in Alabama. She caught tuberculosis and died there as a prisoner.

Brave Lozen is an inspiration to all girls and women. She was not afraid to be different from the other girls. **She is a true rebel and hero!**

"Strong as a man and braver than most. Lozen is a shield to her people."

–Lozen's brother Victorio

strong as a man
braver
than
most

Sarah Loguen Fraser
One of the First Black Female Doctors

Born 1850 in Syracuse, New York
Died 1933 in Washington, DC

Daughter of the Reverend Loguen, Sarah was feisty like her dad. He did not hold back when criticizing slavery, saying, "God made (all men) free."

Sarah was born in the middle of one of the most difficult times in history for African Americans. Her father was a former slave. Slaves were considered "property" of their owners. Both parents were abolitionists (those who wanted slavery to end). The night before her birth, her parents held an important meeting at their home. They met to organize the fight against the Fugitive Slave Act. This was a law that let slave owners go into free states and bring back their "property." To do this was dangerous for Sarah's parents. They could have been sent to prison, but they believed it was worth the risk.

Her home was also a safe house for hundreds of slaves who were using the Underground Railroad. The Underground Railroad was not underground and wasn't actually a train. It was a group of white and free Black people who worked together. They helped runaway slaves escape to freedom in states where slavery was illegal.

By the time Sarah was ten, she knew that standing up for what you believe in is not always popular. But she learned from her parents that helping others is everyone's duty.

She also knew how important education was. When her dad was enslaved, a Methodist family taught him the alphabet and how to discuss his beliefs. Once he was free, he learned to read and write and went to college in New York. He met his wife, Caroline, there. Sarah's parents made sure their children had a good education. They started schools for African Americans in Syracuse, New York.

Sarah was eleven when the Civil War broke out. The Southern states fought to become their own country where they could make laws to keep slavery. The Northern states wanted the US to be united and to outlaw slavery. Several years later, when the war ended, Sarah saw neighbors return. Many were wounded, missing arms or legs, or sick with cholera. The horrors of war had caused some to become mentally ill.

Sarah was a natural caregiver. Her mother got tuberculosis, a disease that had no cure. Sarah took care of her and ran the household when she was still in high school. After her mom died, Sarah took care of the house and helped her dad with his ministry. He died of a heart attack soon after.

Sarah decided to become a doctor after she saw a horrible accident. She was at a railroad station when she noticed a young boy feeding horses between the carriages. She heard screams and horses squealing. A farm wagon had run over the boy, and he was pinned underneath. No one in the crowd knew how to help him and there was no doctor. Sarah vowed, "I will never see a human being in need again and not be able to help."

She went to medical school and applied for internships. An internship is a learning experience in the job you would like to do. Sarah worked at the Woman's Hospital of Philadelphia. She went into areas that were dirty and smelled bad to help poor families. The children she helped nicknamed her Miss Doc. She later went on to become the first female doctor in the Dominican Republic.

For the rest of her life, Sarah lived up to her vow to never see another in need of aid without helping.

"I will never see a human being in need of aid again and not be able to help."

–Sarah Loguen Fraser

I will never, never see a human being in need of aid again
and not be able to help
to help
to help
to help
to he
help
Underground Railroad
Freedom.
Miss Doc
DO GOOD

Emmeline Pankhurst
Hooligan, Rebel, Suffragette

Born 1858 in Manchester, England
Died 1928 in London, England

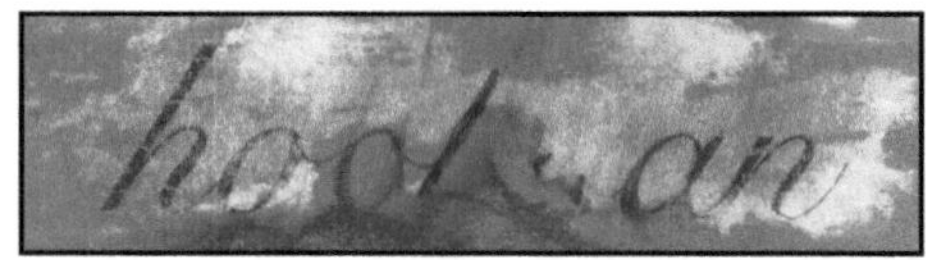

At the turn of the twentieth century, the British had a saying: "The cat, the woman, and the chimney should never leave the house." In those days, women were seen as less important than men. They thought that women were concerned only with what dress or hat to buy and what man to marry and that they should stay home and do embroidery and drink tea.

Luckily for Emmeline, her parents believed strongly in women's rights. As a child, she read newspapers aloud to her father and went to women's suffrage meetings with her mother. They discussed women's right to vote in political elections. At a young age, Emmeline had strong opinions. When she realized her brothers' educations were focused on math, science, and business, while hers was mostly how to keep a nice home and raise a family, she was not happy. Not one bit! "Why should I be expected to wait on the men?" she asked.

At nineteen, she married a lawyer who strongly supported women's rights. She and other women marched, carrying signs and banners to get their message to the people. She was active in suffrage organizations and with other women, organized debates, and passed out flyers and posters, but nothing was changing. Emmeline said it was time to quit talking politely and ACT! She and other women started using the phrase, "Deeds Not Words."

She said, "You have to make more noise than anybody else . . . if you are really going to get your reform realized." Emmeline and the suffragettes began shouting at meetings, using aggressive actions such as chaining themselves to railings, going on hunger strikes, and breaking windows. They often ended up in jail. She said of herself, "I am what you call a hooligan." During Emmeline's time, troublemakers were called hooligans.

Emmeline also was involved in trying to improve working conditions for girls and women. In 1886, she and other women fought for the striking workers at the Bryant and May Match Factory. The girls there worked fourteen hours a day and were fined if they dropped matches on the floor, used the toilet, or talked.

She became a poor law guardian, trying to help people, and was horrified at the living conditions in the workhouses, which were more like prisons for poor people. The people were fed and clothed poorly, and even young kids were forced to scrub floors. She used her voice for improvements and reform in the workhouses. If you've ever seen the movie *Annie*, you have a bit of an idea what these places were like.

In 1928, the year that Emmeline died, women were finally given the same voting rights as men. **Thank goodness for rabble-rousers!**

"*I would rather be a rebel than a slave.*"

–Emmeline Pankhurst

 What word do you see in different parts of the painting? What do you think that word means? Why do you think that word was used to describe Emmeline Pankhurst?

hooligan
hooligan
hooligan
hooligan
hooligan
hooligan

Ida B. Wells
The Courage to Stand Against Injustice

Born 1862 in Holly Springs, Mississippi
Died 1931 in Chicago, Illinois

Ida B. Wells was considered by the FBI to be "one of the most dangerous Negro agitators" (or troublemakers). She spent her life speaking out against many forms of injustice, especially racial prejudice and lack of respect for women.

Ida's parents were enslaved, so when Ida was born during the Civil War, the "master" or slave owner considered her his "property." At age three, when the war ended, her family was freed, and her parents were paid for their work.

Ida was the oldest of eight children. She often took care of her brothers and sisters while her parents worked. She gave them baths and got their clothes ready for Sunday church. If your parents work or you're from a big family, you may have extra responsibilities too! Sadly, at age sixteen, Ida became an orphan. Her parents and baby brother died from the yellow fever epidemic caused by mosquitoes.

As a teen, Ida boarded a train to Nashville with a first-class ticket. However, the railroad had segregated cars and the conductor told her she had to move to the "colored car." Ida refused. The conductor and several passengers dragged her kicking and screaming and ripped the sleeve off her dress. She sued the railroad and won! Her life of activism began on that train.

Three of Ida's friends were lynched (hanged) for owning a grocery store that was in competition with a white-owned grocery. She exposed the truth and urged Black people to boycott white-owned businesses. The authorities warned her to stop, but she continued to speak out. They also told her that she would be killed on sight, so she moved to New York City. There she spoke about the horrors of lynching in the South.

In 1895, she married Ferdinand Barnett and hyphenated her last name to Wells-Barnett, which was very unusual back then. Ida was strong and fierce and wanted the world to know it!

In Chicago, she founded the first Black suffrage club and started the first Black kindergarten. Always unafraid to speak up, Ida visited President McKinley and asked him to treat lynchings as a federal crime.

In 1913, women from all over the country planned a march on Washington to achieve voting rights for all women. Ida joined them, but the organizer told her that only white women could represent Illinois at the front of the line. They said Black women had to march separately at the end of the parade. Ida's thoughts were basically, "Are you kidding me?!" And she left the room.

Suddenly, as the parade continued, Ida moved in from the sidelines. She marched with the white women while two of them held her hands in support. No one stops Ida!

As Ida said, "Let the truth be told." **Ida always refused to be silent.**

"The way to right wrongs is to shed the light of Truth upon them."
–Ida B. Wells

Let the truth be told.
Stay woke.
The courage to stand against injustice.
The way to right wrongs is to shed the light of Truth upon them.

Zitkala-Sa (Redbird)

Fighter for Women and the Rights of Native Americans

Born 1876 in South Dakota
Died 1938 in Washington, DC

For the Sioux tribe, "short hair was worn by cowards." When enemies captured warriors, their hair was cut off. Imagine Redbird's shame when her long braids were cut off by white teachers at her school. She hid from them to avoid this, but they found her. In her words, "I felt the cold blades of the scissors against my neck and heard them gnaw off one of my thick braids. Then I lost my spirit."

Zitkala-Sa was born Gertrude Simmons on the Yankton Sioux Reservation in South Dakota. Her dad was French, and her mom was Sioux. Her dad left when she was very young. When she was eight, Quaker missionaries came to her home to bring her and seven other children to their boarding school. They promised the kids as many red apples as they could eat, a train ride, and an education. She felt happy. But on the train, she started to feel scared and alone. She noticed that the white passengers stared at the moccasins and blankets they wore.

At the school in Indiana, everything was so different from what she was used to. The sounds of heavy shoes on a wooden floor felt harsh and frightening. She grew up outdoors, surrounded by the sounds of birds, rippling water, and the sweet smell of flowers.

She struggled with how she felt about her new life. On the one hand, she was grateful. She learned to read and write and how to play the violin. The Quakers taught her about equal rights for women and tolerance for all people. They taught her how important it was to fight against injustice. But after three years at the school, she returned home to her mom. She realized that the Quakers didn't truly understand the importance of Native American culture. When they took young kids away from their families, they made them lose their language and traditions.

Gertrude felt like she was in the middle of two worlds. She wanted to honor her heritage. But she also wanted more education. She loved to learn and loved music, so she returned to the white institute again. At age fifteen, Gertrude changed her name to Zitkala-Sa, which means Redbird. She was such a talented violin player that when the music teacher left, Redbird was hired to take her place.

After that, her mom wanted her to come back to the reservation. She decided not to, so she could continue her education at Earlham College. But she felt lonely, missed her mom, and cried in secret. She felt like the other students weren't friendly. She decided to stick it out and entered a speech contest. She spoke about women's rights and the right to vote. Her classmates cheered her on and shouted her name. She felt then that she had made the right decision. She won first place and the local newspaper declared her speech "a masterpiece."

She returned to her homeland and married a Yankton Sioux man. They went to Washington, DC, to fight for the rights of Native Americans. She worked for Native Americans to gain US citizenship and regain control of their lives. **Zitkala-Sa feared no man and fought for her people until she died.**

"*I fear no man.*"

—Zitkala-Sa (Redbird)

LOOK AT THE PAINTING Gertrude Simmons chose the name Zitkala-Sa (which means Redbird). Why do you think she chose a bird? What can birds do that humans can't?

I fear no man. I fear no man.
I fear no man. I fear no man.
Vocal proponent for women
and voting rights for women
and activist. Vocal proponent
languages

Alice Paul

Feminist Fighter for Women's Right to Vote

Born 1885 in New Jersey
Died 1977 in New Jersey

Alice Paul grew up as a Quaker. Quakers also called themselves Friends. They believed that anyone could talk to God on their own without a minister. The Quakers believed in gender equality (that boys and girls were equal), so she and her brothers did the same work on their parents' farm. She played tennis with her brothers and sisters, checkers on the big porch, and read in the library. As a Quaker, her life was peaceful.

In school, Alice loved to be active. She was good at basketball, baseball, and field hockey, and loved to dance and ice-skate. At the time, these sports were mostly for boys. Do you think that stopped Alice? No way!

Her mom was curious about women's suffrage (women's right to vote) and took Alice with her to suffrage meetings at her friend's homes. Alice learned that many people thought women were not equal to men and they definitely didn't think women should have the right to vote.

Imagine if your class was voting for class president. You really want your friend to win. But when you try to vote, the teacher says only kids with blue eyes can vote, and yours are brown. Does this rule make sense? Of course not, but that's what it was like for women before 1920. If you were a woman, you weren't allowed to vote.

Alice went to college, then studied in England, where she became an activist, a person who works to bring social change. One of her first acts of defiance was sneaking into a political banquet with her friend, dressed as maids with mops and brooms. From the second-floor balcony, her friend smashed a window with her shoe, and the two yelled out, "Votes for Women!"

Alice returned to the United States to continue her work. Alice and her suffragist friends were jailed many times and went on hunger strikes. They organized to picket the White House with signs demanding suffrage for women. Finally, in 1918 President Wilson agreed to allow women to vote, but it took two more years for it to be approved by at least thirty-six states.

Alice Paul, the little Quaker girl from a peaceful childhood, became a force to be reckoned with. She inspired women to stand tall, be brave, and demand freedom. **Thank you, mighty Alice!**

 It says, "Deeds not words." A deed is an action. What do you think that means?

"Mr. President, how long must women wait to get their liberty? Let us have the rights we deserve."
—Alice Paul

Deeds not words
Equal
not words
Deeds
liberty
No punishment
desire liberty
prevent those who

Frida Kahlo

Feminist Rebel Artist

Born 1907 in Mexico City, Mexico
Died 1954 in Mexico City, Mexico

Frida was born in La Casa Azul (The Blue House), which her dad had built in Mexico. She was very curious about nature and science. She brought home insects, frogs, and plants to study. But when she was only six, Frida caught polio. She had to stay in her room for nine months! She was bored, so she made up an imaginary friend to keep her company. Her friend's name was also Frida, and this friend was able to dance and play.

The polio caused her right leg to become thin and weaker. But Frida did not let that stop her. She played soccer, wrestled, boxed, and was an excellent swimmer. At that time, Mexican girls didn't usually do these things. But Frida refused to worry about what others expected her to do. She was a rebel.

Frida was very smart and was a whiz at math and science. She wanted to become a doctor. She also loved having fun with her friends and was daring and brave.

But at age eighteen, Frida was riding the bus home from high school. A streetcar hit the bus and Frida was trapped inside. A piece of metal from the bus speared through her spine. She had to be in a full-body plaster cast and be still. Poor Frida! This was torture for such an energetic and daring girl. After this, Frida was in pain for the rest of her life. Her dream of becoming a doctor was ended.

Frida borrowed her dad's paints and painted butterflies on her body cast. Her parents gave her a special easel so that she could paint from her bed. She used a mirror and painted herself because she was alone so much. Frida painted different versions of herself. She wanted to show what it felt like to be many different people in one body. When she was happy, her paintings were filled with bright colors, plants, and animals. When she was sad, her paintings were darker. Some people thought her paintings looked like nightmares. Frida answered, "I paint my own reality. I turn my pain into beauty."

During her lifetime in Mexico, only men became famous artists. She married a famous Mexican artist Diego Rivera, who painted murals on walls. But Frida was the first Mexican woman to have her own art exhibit in New York City. She also was the first to have her art in the Louvre Museum in Paris.

Strong, stubborn, and curious, Frida was not afraid to be herself. In her self-portraits, she emphasized her thick, bushy eyebrows and bit of a mustache. She was proud of how she looked and didn't care that she wasn't perfect!

Frida painted to help herself get through tough times. Her paintings helped many women and girls find strength in their own struggles with pain or suffering. Frida had a favorite saying. **"Viva La Vida!" Long Live Life! She truly lived life to the fullest and never gave up. Viva La Frida!**

"I turn my pain into beauty."
—Frida Kahlo

 Frida experienced much pain and injury in her life. In this painting of Frida, what words do you see? What do you think Frida meant by these words? Have you ever broken a leg or gotten hurt and felt pain? If so, what did you do to feel better?

turn pain into beauty....
I paint my own reality
turn pain into
beauty
FEMINIST
I paint my own reality
turn pain into beauty
...turn pain into beauty
...turn pain into beauty
...turn pain into beauty
paint reality

Rosa Parks

First Lady of Civil Rights

Born 1913 near Montgomery, Alabama
Died 2005 in Detroit, Michigan

When Rosa was born, segregation was everywhere in the United States, but in the South more than anywhere. That meant that Black people and white people couldn't attend the same schools, use the same bathrooms, drinking fountains, or swimming pools. If Black people wanted to eat in a restaurant, they had to enter through back doors, order through hidden hatches, and sit in a separate area. Sometimes they weren't allowed in at all.

Can you imagine a hot summer's day in the South, with no air-conditioning, and you walk by a pool full of splashing kids cooling off and you want to join them? Oh wait, you can't because you're Black.

When Rosa was only two, her parents split up. She and her mom and little brother went to live on a farm with her grandparents, who had been enslaved people. They believed there should be equal rights for both Black and white people.

Her grandfather Sylvester inspired her to stand up for herself. He would sit on the front porch with a shotgun to protect his family from the Ku Klux Klan, who were lynching (hanging) innocent Black people. When Rosa was ten, a white boy named Franklin threatened to hit her. Rosa wasn't having it! She picked up a brick and drew her arm back to defend herself. He walked away. This was the first time Rosa stood up for herself, but it wouldn't be the last!

Rosa's mom, a teacher, taught her to read at an early age, and when she got to school, she studied hard. Her school did not have the supplies, books, and many of the things the white schools provided. At age sixteen, Rosa had to quit school to care for her grandmother and mother who were ill. It wasn't until she married her husband, Raymond, at age nineteen, that she was able to finish and graduate from high school. Raymond was a member of the civil rights group NAACP, the National Association for the Advancement of Colored People. This group was formed to respond to the violence against Black people. Rosa was the first woman to join.

One of the things Rosa hated the most was the unfair bus system. Black people had to enter the bus from the front, pay their fare, then exit and reenter from the back. At times, the driver would take their money and drive away without letting them back on.

After a long day's work in 1955, Rosa boarded the bus to go home. Rosa was told to stand so that a white man could take her seat. No way was she going to let THAT happen! The bus driver called the police, and they arrested Rosa and put her in jail. Many people agreed with Rosa that this was unfair, so they decided to boycott, or avoid the buses. The NAACP and Martin Luther King Jr. joined this peaceful protest, which lasted for 381 days. Finally, the Supreme Court ruled against this bus segregation law. Their hard work had paid off!

Rosa continued her work for civil rights, earning the Congressional Gold Medal and the Presidential Medal of Freedom. In 1999, *Time* magazine named Rosa Parks one of the twenty most powerful and influential figures of the twentieth century.

Rosa and her husband were never able to have children of their own, but it's no wonder brave Rosa was called the Mother of the Freedom Movement!

LOOK AT THE PAINTING What phrase is repeated in the background and on Rosa's shirt? As a Black person, Rosa was sick of being treated like she wasn't as important or worthy of respect as white people. Have you ever been in a situation where you did not feel seen or respected? What did you do?

reme Court Outlaws Bus Segregati
tters Instructed To End Car Pool
NEGROES TO CONTINUE BOYC
no, the only tir
My tired I was, was tired of giving in
7053
tired

"From the time I was a child, I tried to protest against disrespectful treatment."
—Rosa Parks

Edie Windsor

Early Activist for LGBTQ Rights

Born 1929 in Philadelphia, Pennsylvania
Died 2017 in New York, New York

Edie was born in 1929, the youngest child of Russian-Jewish immigrants. Immigrants are people who leave their country to live in another country, hoping for a better life. Her father owned a candy and ice cream store in a poor area of town, and they lived above it. Sounds like a dream come true to have all that ice cream and candy so close, doesn't it? But when Edie was only two, she and her brother got polio, and the store had to be quarantined (closed down to stop germs from spreading).

Edie remembers her dad learning how to speak English from a dictionary. He made sure Edie had books to read, and she loved that. She also remembers her mom telling her that if a boy called her "a dirty Jew," she should pull his hair and run home. This is how Edie learned what anti-Semitism is. Anti-Semitism is when Jewish people are discriminated against because of their religion.

Edie's family later moved to a middle-class neighborhood. Her mom said it was so that her daughters would meet the right boys. Edie always dated boys, and many fell in love with her. She had crushes on girls but didn't know why. She had no idea what gay was.

When Edie was a teen and young adult, people hid their true feelings because being gay was not accepted at all. In fact, it was illegal. When she graduated from college in 1950, the laws would not allow gay people to get a job or buy a house. The laws said gay people were criminals. Very few people admitted to being gay because of that. Some, like Edie, married a man because in the 1950s women were supposed to count on their husbands to support them. A year later, Edie got a divorce.

Edie knew she needed to support herself. She got her master's degree in math and got a job at a prestigious global technology company. She was so bright that she achieved the highest technical job at the company. But all along, she was terrified of them finding out she was gay.

In 1965, she began dating her partner, Thea Spyer. They had to keep their relationship secret because it was illegal. In 1977, Thea became very ill and could no longer walk. Finally, in 2007, they were able to marry in Canada. Sadly, Thea died two years later. They had no rights as a couple by law in the US, but Edie challenged the law and won her case in the Supreme Court. Two years later, the court ruled in favor of marriage equality for all.

Edie won countless awards for her activism and was nominated for *Time* magazine's Person of the Year. **Edie helped so many people because she never gave up!**

LOOK AT THE PAINTING When Edie won her court case for equal rights for gay couples, she opened her arms wide in celebration on the steps of the Supreme Court. Do you see other outstretched hands in the painting? What do those hands mean to you?

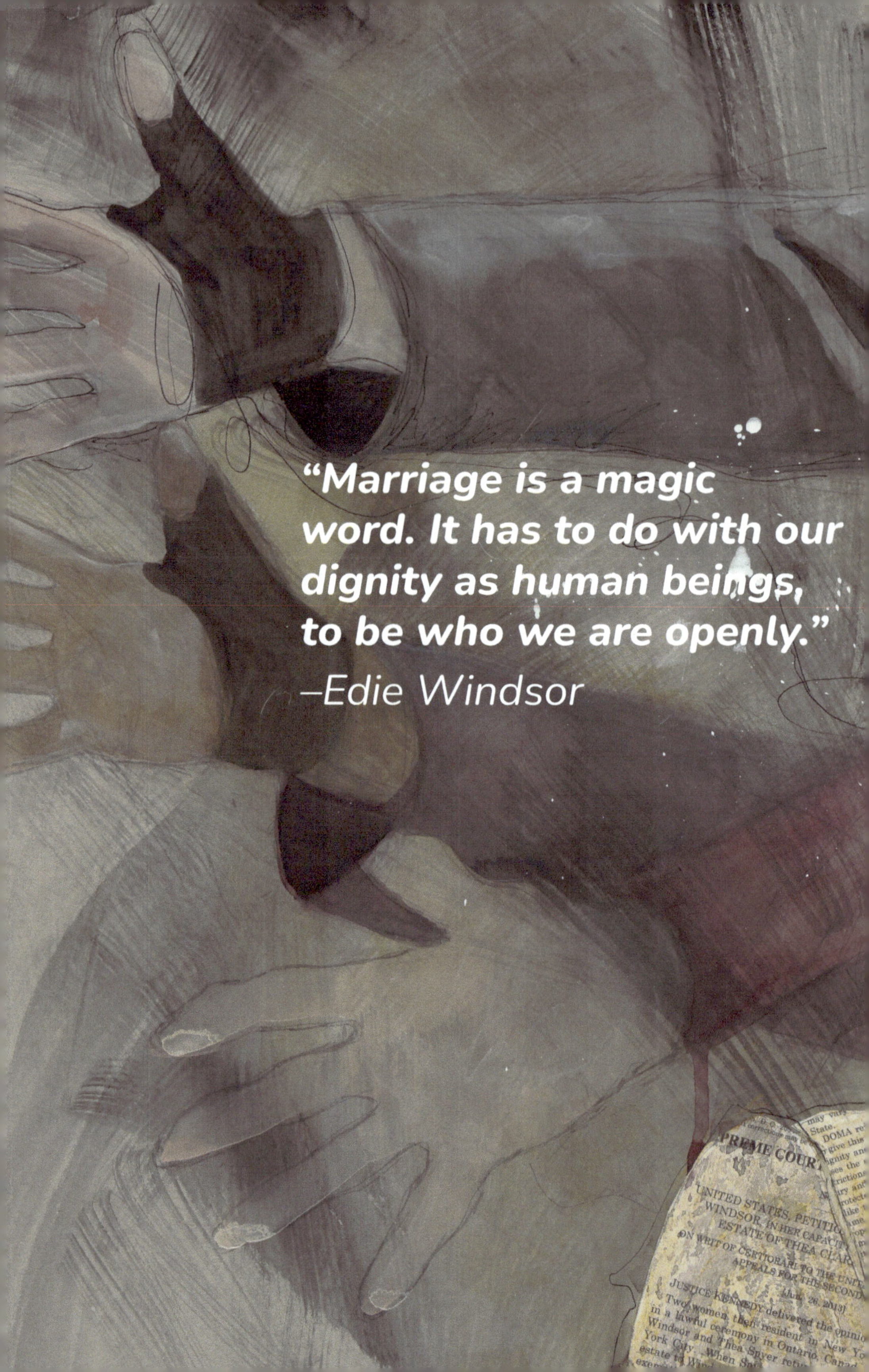

"Marriage is a magic word. It has to do with our dignity as human beings, to be who we are openly."
—Edie Windsor

transgender

Ruth Bader Ginsburg
A Fearless Voice for Equality and Justice

Born in 1933 in Brooklyn, New York
Died in 2020 in Washington, DC

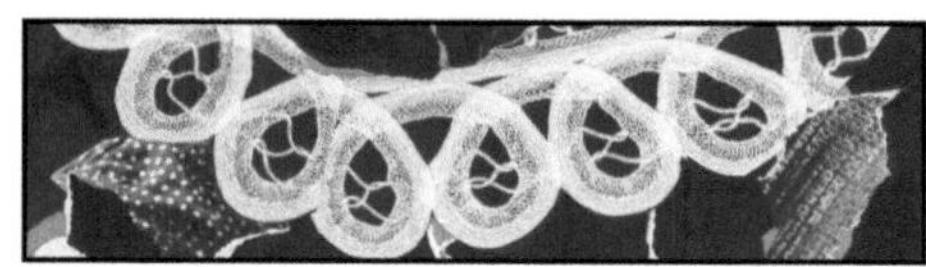

Ruth was a popular symbol of justice, perseverance, and female empowerment. Her hair bun, glasses, and lace collars became famous as symbols. She was a tiny woman but a huge force on the Supreme Court.

Ruth was born in low-income, working-class Brooklyn. Her father was a Jewish immigrant from Ukraine, and her mom was born in New York to Jewish parents from Poland. Her mom worked in a garment factory, but was a major influence in Ruth's life. She taught Ruth the value of independence and a good education. Sadly, when Ruth was a teen, her mom struggled with cancer. Ruth would sit by her side and do her homework to spend time with her.

Ruth said, "My mother told me to be a lady and to be independent." For her that meant being your own person. The day before Ruth graduated from high school, her mom died.

At Cornell University, Ruth met her husband, Marty. Ruth said, "Marty was the first boy I met who cared that I had a brain." They got married and their first child was born just as he was drafted into the army. Their marriage was one of equality; they worked as a team.

Ruth learned to balance life as a mom and a law student in a very male-dominated environment. In studying law, Ruth was a pioneer for women of her generation. "For most girls growing up in the 1940s, the most important degree was not your BA but your MRS." In other words, it was assumed that women only wanted to become a wife, not get their college degree. Ruth did NOT agree!

Ruth was one of only nine women at Harvard Law School. In 1956, the dean asked her and the other eight women why they were taking up seats that should have been filled by men! Whaaaat?! Ruth tied for first in her class and was recommended for a clerkship with a Supreme Court justice. He said he wasn't ready to hire a woman! Ridiculous, thought Ruth!

"Ginsburg comes from the generation of women who had to be three times better than men to get half the recognition," said author Katherine Franke.

After finally getting hired in 1963, she had to fight for equal pay. She fought and won five major Supreme Court cases in the 1970s. Ruth was fighting for what should have been obvious: women were fully equal to men. She got that made into a law. In 1993, she became the second woman ever to serve on the US Supreme Court.

By 2013, Ruth was so popular that she was given a new nickname, The Notorious RBG. This funny name is a twist on the nickname of rapper Biggie Smalls, The Notorious BIG. She liked this new name and had T-shirts made with it.

Though she spoke softly, she was fierce. During her lifetime, people called Ruth a "pint-sized powerhouse." She never let her tiny size hold her back. **When she died in 2020, the world lost a giant.**

"Fight for the things you care about. But do it in a way that will lead others to join you."

–Ruth Bader Ginsburg

Friends of the Earth
WOMAN'S PLACE IS IN THE RESISTANCE
CHALLENGING INEQUALITY
NOTORIUS

Audre Lorde

Poet, Feminist, and Equal rights Advocate

Born 1934 in Harlem, New York
Died 1992 in Virgin Islands

When people asked eight-year-old Audre how she was doing, she would answer with a poem she had memorized. Audre loved reading and writing. She couldn't always find a poem that described her feelings. So, at age eight, she wrote her own poetry.

Audre's parents were immigrants from Grenada, an island in the Caribbean Sea. They came to Harlem, New York, and that is where Audre was born. Harlem had been a place of great creativity, where singers, musicians, artists, and writers worked. But a year after Audre was born, it was a place of poverty, protests, and crowded conditions.

Audre described her childhood as unsettled. Her mom was light skinned and wasn't happy that her daughter's skin was darker. Her father was cold and distant. Audre was ashamed that she was dark skinned.

Audre continued to love writing and was an excellent student. An English teacher rejected a poem she wrote, but Audre did not give up. She submitted it to *Seventeen* magazine and it was published! She dropped the *Y* from her first name, Audrey, because she felt more like Audre. Even as a teen, she knew who she was.

After high school graduation, she went on a trip to Mexico. In Mexico, Audre felt accepted as both a Black and gay woman. Her confidence in herself grew. She realized that she had been silent about feeling ashamed. She decided to use her voice to express herself with confidence.

Audre returned to the US and got her bachelor's degree from Hunter College. She then went to Columbia University and earned her master's degree in library science. She worked as a librarian in the New York City public schools for the next seven years. During that time, in the '60s, the civil rights movement was in full swing. Audre used her voice and writing to speak about civil rights, which include protection against being treated differently from others. She also spoke out against the Vietnam War and for women's liberation. Women's liberation is about women having the same rights as men to determine their own lives. This is what being a feminist is all about.

She continued to write poetry and books during the '70s and '80s, winning many honors. In 1977, she was diagnosed with breast cancer. The treatments and surgery were very hard on her, and she wrote about her pain in a book called *The Cancer Journals*. She wanted to help others who were going through a cancer experience. At that time, people did not speak about their cancer and often felt alone when dealing with it. She became a dedicated advocate for those without a voice.

Just before her death, she had an African naming ceremony. She chose a new name, Gamba Adisa. It means Warrior: She Who Makes Her Meaning Known. How awesome is that to have a name that describes her so perfectly!

"Your silence will not protect you."

—Audre Lorde

 Do you see the words, "when we are silent, we are still afraid, so it is better to speak"? If you've ever been bullied or know someone who has, being silent about it won't make it go away. Can you think of any time when it is better to speak up than stay quiet?

it is
better to speak
Women are powerful and danger
It is not our differences that divide us
We must be the change we wish to see in the world.
It is not our differences that divide us.

Gloria Steinem
Leader of the
Women's Rights Movement

Born 1934 in Toledo, Ohio

Gloria Steinem was a trailblazer and feminist. A trailblazer is someone who is willing to take risks and go on a path that isn't already there. A feminist believes all genders should have equal rights and opportunities. Seems like common sense, doesn't it? But in the 1950s and '60s, that's not the way it was! In the 1960s, these are some things women weren't allowed to do:

1. Apply for a credit card without her husband's signature.

2. Serve on a jury in court.

3. Use birth control.

4. Attend Ivy League colleges like Harvard or Yale.

5. Be a stewardess on a plane if married. Also had to be a certain height, weight, must have "soft hands" and retire by age thirty-two. Whaaaat!?

Gloria's childhood was not easy. She was born during the Depression, a time when many lost their jobs and money. Right before Gloria's birth, her mom had a nervous breakdown and was unable to care for Gloria and her sister. The family traveled around the country in a trailer while her father sold antiques from it. During this time, Gloria and her sister missed out on a lot of school and having school friends. After her sister left for college, Gloria spent a lot of time on her own at her father's resort in Michigan. She played on the beach, catching turtles and little fish.

When she was ten, her parents divorced. Gloria then lived with her mom in Toledo and took care of her. She finally got to go to school every day! When she was a senior in high school, she moved to live with her sister in Washington, DC. After graduation, she attended Smith College and loved it. She was able to focus on her schoolwork for the first time in her life.

Gloria became a journalist, but her male bosses wanted her to write only about beauty and fashion. That was NOT Gloria's plan! She wanted to write about important issues like poverty, lack of childcare, and equal rights. Along with other feminists, Gloria started the National Women's Political Caucus in 1971. This helped women to run for political offices. Then they would have a voice in what laws were passed.

That same year, she started *Ms.* magazine, the first national feminist magazine for women's issues. Men had been in charge of both the newspapers and magazines. Gloria wanted women to have a voice, so she decided to start her own. Turns out, people wanted to find out what women had to say. It was a huge success! Go Ms. Steinem!

Steinem famously said, "A woman needs a man like a fish needs a bicycle." But at age sixty-six, Gloria married. Though she worked for equality in marriage, she never expected to get married herself. She said, "Feminism is about the ability to choose what's right at each time of our lives."

Even in her late 80s, she continues her passion for women's issues and equal rights for all.

"We are the women our parents warned us against, and we are proud."

–Gloria Steinem

THE TRUTH WILL SET YOU FREE
BUT FIRST IT WILL PISS YOU OFF
UNITED WOMEN'S CONTINGENT
WOMANPOWER
On Washington Against the War

Aretha Franklin

Queen of Soul

Born 1942 in Memphis, Tennessee
Died 2018 in Detroit, Michigan

As a little girl, Aretha was extremely shy and close to her mom. Her mom was a gospel singer and pianist. Her dad was a famous Baptist preacher but with a violent temper. Her parents' relationship was a stormy one, so her mom left when Aretha was six years old. Aretha's heart was broken after that. Though she got to visit her mom, Aretha was so sad that she became withdrawn. Then, when she was only ten, her mom died suddenly of a heart attack. Aretha stopped speaking for weeks.

As a child, Aretha taught herself how to play the piano. She never learned to read music but had a natural gift for it. She was considered a child prodigy (an exceptional talent). Music is what helped her cope with her sadness.

Aretha had her first child at age twelve and another at age fourteen. Since she was still a child herself, this was very difficult. Her grandmother and her sister helped care for these children. Her childhood inspired her soulful and powerful music.

When she was young, Aretha participated in meetings at her home with Martin Luther King Jr. and other famous Black leaders.

They were talking about how to improve Black Americans' lives. Her father brought her along on his traveling gospel-singing tours. She recorded her first gospel album, *Songs of Faith*, at age fourteen. She even got to sing at Martin Luther King's civil rights tours when she was sixteen. Her voice was that amazing!

In 1960, at age eighteen, Aretha moved to New York. She wanted to sing more than just gospel; she wanted to sing soul, jazz, and rhythm and blues. The 1960s were full of unrest. People were marching to demand racial equality. They marched to protest the Vietnam War. It was during these times that Aretha recorded "Respect." It was a demand for equality and freedom. That song became the anthem (or melody) for both the civil rights and women's Movements. After her hit song "Respect," Aretha was crowned the "Queen of Soul."

Aretha recorded 112 singles. She performed in many concerts to raise money for civil rights groups. She won eighteen Grammys and was the first woman inducted into the Rock and Roll Hall of Fame. She sang at Martin Luther King Jr.'s funeral. She sang for Queen Elizabeth and at President Obama's inauguration.

Aretha's songs told stories, both sad and happy. Even as a young girl, she was able to use her voice to give her strength during hard times. The trauma (suffering) of her childhood inspired her soulful and powerful music. **The Queen of Soul was a Survivor.**

LOOK AT THE PAINTING What things in the painting show that Aretha was a singer? She was shy but used her voice to demand equal rights for both Black and white people. You may not be an amazing singer like Aretha, but have you ever used your voice to say something important?

spect
Res
"They say it's a mar
But you
spect when you come home

All I'm ask - ing   is for a lit - tle re -
spect when you come home.
"We all require and want respect, man or woman, black or white. It's our basic human right."
—Aretha Franklin
respect
ove that by me   "

Temple Grandin
The Scientist who Thought in Pictures

Born 1947 in Boston, Massachusetts

Temple was an unusual baby. When her young mother, Eustacia, tried to hug her, she didn't like it. She acted wild and clawed at her mom. She would flap her hands and make peeping sounds. She broke her toys and tore wallpaper off walls. She chewed puzzle pieces and spit them out. Then other days she would be fine. Her mom worried that it was her fault. It wasn't.

Doctors suggested she live in a hospital for children with mental problems. Her father agreed. Her mom wasn't having it. In the 1940s, not much was known about her condition. It is called autism. It affects the way a person acts. Some never learn to speak and are in their own world. Others grow up to lead happy, successful lives, though they may be unusual.

When she was three, her mom took her to a special brain doctor called a neurologist. The tests he did on her showed she was extremely smart. Temple went to speech therapy and learned to talk. By age five, she turned into a chatterbox and wouldn't stop!

Kids with autism are often very sensitive to loud noises, bright lights, strong smells, and rough fabrics. When these things become too much, that is when a tantrum happens. Temple so wanted to fit in and, when she didn't, would sometimes have a meltdown. She flinched at the slightest touch but secretly wanted to be hugged. Imagine what that would feel like!

54

As a child, Temple was a good artist and could invent and build things herself. She explained that she "thought in pictures." She would picture something in her mind, draw it, and build it. Temple said, "Art was always encouraged in our home. Art was what saved me."

Because of her autism, Temple had a hard time knowing how to be social. In middle school, she was bullied. She acted differently than the other kids. Loud sounds like the school bell scared her. She repeated things over and over loudly. Now that the kids she knew were older, they cared more about things like clothes, boys, and music. Temple didn't care about these things. She also didn't understand jokes or sarcasm like "Yeah right" when you really mean "not a chance!" The insults and name-calling were too much. Talk about MEAN GIRLS! Temple threw a book at one of the name-callers. The principal expelled her.

Temple's mom found a small country school where Temple would live during high school. It had horses and a farm. She spent all of her free time in the stables. She became an excellent rider and could calm even the wildest horse! She made friends but still didn't understand why they cared about hair and makeup. But as she became a young woman and her body changed, she began having panic attacks. How could she make them stop?

At age fifteen, on her aunt's ranch in Arizona, she discovered her answer. She watched the cows getting their shots from the vet. They went into a chute where the sides pressed in on their bodies. This calmed them down. Could this be how hugs worked? Temple tried it and it felt relaxing! She built a hug machine and used it whenever a panic attack came.

She went on to college and got her PhD. Temple used her skills and compassion to help animals and others with autism. She knew what it was like to have anxiety and understood how the cattle felt. She helped farm animals to be treated in a gentler way. The girl who didn't speak as a child went on to be a speaker all over the world. She is now a professor of animal science at Colorado State University.

By the way, when her hug machine broke, she realized what she really wanted was a hug from her mom. In her words, "I'm into hugging people now."

"I am different, not less."

—Temple Grandin

 In my painting, I have included words from Temple herself. What do you think they mean? Do you think being different is good or bad? Have you ever felt different?

56

I am
different,
not
less.

Ellen Ochoa

First Latina Astronaut to Fly into Space

Born 1958 in Los Angeles, California

Ellen Ochoa's grandparents were Mexican immigrants. Her dad remembers what it was like as a child when the family moved to Arizona. He and his friends were not allowed to use the public swimming pool. This was hard because Arizona gets very hot. They could only use the pool the day before it was cleaned. People thought the immigrants were dirty. Imagine how that made them feel!

Ellen was the middle of five children. Her dad did not want the children to speak Spanish. He was afraid they would be looked down on. Her dad joined the navy. Her mom was home with the kids. However, when Ellen was a baby, her mom started college. She wanted to set a good example for her kids.

Ellen loved to read, but her favorite subject was math. She did well in school. She even won her county's spelling bee when she was thirteen. She also loved music and started playing the flute when she was ten.

When Ellen was in middle school, her parents divorced. This was a difficult time for her. She put all her energy into music and school. She graduated from high school as class valedictorian. A valedictorian is the student with the highest grades in her class. She also gave the farewell speech at graduation.

Ellen studied physics at San Diego State University and again was valedictorian when she graduated. She still loved music and played her flute. But she received a scholarship to Stanford to study engineering. There were only a few women in her classes, but Ellen didn't care. She went on to get her doctorate and studied optics. Optics are the science of sight and light. She invented three optical systems and got patents for each.

In 1983, Sally Ride was the first female astronaut. Ellen was inspired by this. "She helped me picture myself as an astronaut, which seemed like an impossible dream," said Ellen. She applied to the NASA Astronaut Training Program but did not get in. At the time, most astronauts had their pilot's license. She continued her work developing computer systems for space. But she also earned her pilot's license. This got her a step closer.

On her third try, Ellen was accepted into the training program. She and her husband moved to Houston so that she could train at the Johnson Space Center. Part of the program was learning astronomy, the study of stars, planets, the sun, and moon. She also had to be in top physical shape and learn survival skills.

In 1993, Ellen went on her first mission aboard the space shuttle Discovery. She went on to spend one thousand hours in space. She even played her flute in space! She became the first Hispanic director of the Johnson Space Center.

In interviews, Dr. Ochoa said, "You don't have to wait until you're older to make an impact on other people's lives. Science is all around us, and children are born with a keen desire to explore, making them natural scientists."

Ellen Ochoa did not give up on her dream when she didn't get chosen the first two times for astronaut training. **She just kept on learning and her dream came true!**

"Don't be afraid to reach for the stars."

—Ellen Ochoa

LOOK AT THE PAINTING Though Ellen Ochoa was an astronaut and scientist, she had other interests as well. Can you find one of them in the painting? You may be very good at something, but are there other things that interest you? Why do you think that's important?

be afraid to reach for the stars. I believe a good education can take y
h and beyond." "Don't be afraid to reach for the stars. I believe a g
"Don't be afraid to reach for the stars. I believe a good education c
on Earth and beyond." "Don't be afraid to reach for the stars. I belie
Desire to Discover
Motivation
Perseverance
Don't be afraid to reach for the stars
ELLEN OCHOA
NASA

Simone Biles
The Most Talented Gymnast of All Time

Born 1997 in Columbus, Ohio

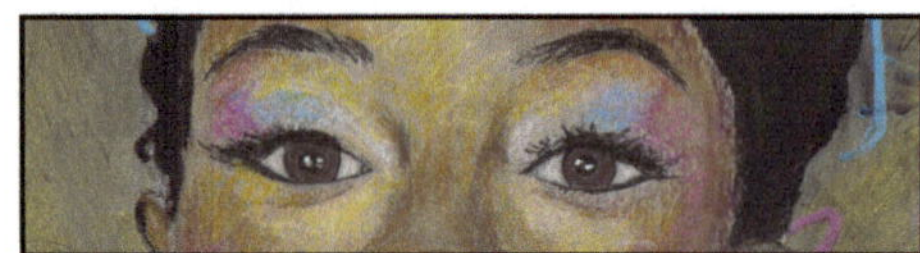

Small but mighty. A tiny powerhouse. Daredevil. These are just a few of the words that describe her. Despite being only four feet, eight inches, Simone Biles is considered one of the greatest athletes in history. She has won twenty-five world medals in gymnastics. Nineteen of these were gold, the most in gymnastics history! She is known and admired throughout the world. But things were not always this wonderful.

Her parents struggled with drug and alcohol addiction, and her father abandoned the family when Simone was three years old. She and her little sister, Adria, were put into foster care. Her mom's dad and his second wife adopted them, and another aunt adopted the two older siblings. They gave the girls the security of a safe home in Texas. Simone considers them her parents.

Adria called Simone "fearless." When she was very young, Simone would jump off a second-floor railing onto a sofa one floor below. She also taught herself to flip backward off of mailboxes. OK, readers, DO NOT TRY THIS AT HOME! Simone discovered gymnastics at age six on a day-care field trip. She began imitating the moves. The instructor encouraged her parents to enroll her in gymnastics. She started training with coach Aimee Boorman at age eight.

Simone had boundless energy that made her such a good athlete. But at school, it was difficult for her to sit still and learn. Her doctors prescribed Ritalin for her ADHD (attention deficit hyperactivity disorder). This helped her to focus at school and gymnastics. Simone later said, "My challenge is also my superpower: ADHD."

At age fourteen, Simone had to make a difficult decision. She decided to leave her public school to be homeschooled, so she could compete as a gymnast. This meant she gave up a lot of fun activities. She began competing and was doing very well until she lost control on the balance beam and fell in 2013. She went to a sports psychologist and learned how to stop worrying about what others expected. By age sixteen, she had won two gold medals. She went on to begin an amazing winning streak!

But in 2016, Russian hackers discovered that Simone had ADHD and took Ritalin. It is a banned substance for athletes, but Simone has permission to take it. She sent out a message on Twitter that taking meds for ADHD is nothing to be ashamed of. She encouraged other girls to "Use your voice. Courage is your superpower."

Not only was Simone talented, she was also TOUGH! After spending the night in the ER with a painful kidney stone, she helped lead Team USA to first place in the World Artistic Gymnastics Championships the next day.

Simone isn't only about work though. She orders pepperoni pizza after every meet. She also is crazy about her two dogs, Lilo and Rambo. She says they help her cope with pressure. To inspire other girls to be confident, she started a line of clothing for Athleta. She says there are hidden notes in every piece of clothing. "I want kids to feel comfortable and confident in not only what they wear but also in their own skin." Her favorite color is yellow and she's afraid of bees. Hey, she's human!

There is another way we know super Simone is human. At the 2020 Tokyo Olympics, she was so stressed out that she decided to leave the Olympics and take care of her mental health. She spoke out about taking a break when you need it and to not be ashamed of that. **She is not only a champion gymnast, but a champion for mental health too.**

"Courage is your superpower. Use your voice."
—Simone Biles

LOOK AT THE PAINTING When you look at the painting, you will see some of Simone's favorite sayings. What are they? What do you think they meant to her? What do they mean to you?

Courage is your superpower.
Use your voice
Courage is your superpower.
Use your voice.
Courage is your superpower.
Courage is your superpower.
Use your voice.
Courage is your superpower.
Use your voice.
Use your voice
Use your voice

Naomi Osaka

One of the World's Greatest Tennis Players

Born 1997 in Osaka, Japan

How many three-year-olds do you know who can play tennis? Naomi Osaka was just that age when she started playing!

Naomi was born in Osaka, Japan. Her dad, Leonard, and her mom, Tamaki, met in Japan during college. Her father is from Haiti. Tamaki's parents did not approve of the relationship because Leonard was not Japanese. They got married anyway. Sadly, they had no contact with Tamaki's parents for almost ten years.

During that time, Mari, Naomi's older sister, and Naomi were born. In their home, they spoke English, Japanese, and Creole, their father's language. Then Leonard saw sisters Serena and Venus Williams playing tennis in the French Open. He got an idea. He would teach his daughters to become great tennis players too!

The family moved to New York when Naomi was three. They stayed with Leonard's parents there. Their dad started them on a strict schedule of tennis instruction. They went to gyms, public courts, watched DVDs and read about tennis. He made them hit one thousand balls each day!

The sisters practiced every day, but Naomi always lost to her older sister. Each day, Naomi would tell Mari, "I'm going to beat you tomorrow." That took twelve years, but she never gave up. While in New York, they had the best of both worlds. They loved eating the delicious Creole food their grandma made. They also got to enjoy their mom, Tamaki's Japanese food.

When Naomi was nine, the family moved to Florida, so they could play tennis year-round. Money was tight, so Tamaki worked to help pay for professional coaching. At first, the pro coaches weren't sure how good Naomi was. But then they saw her run—really FAST! They knew she could cover the court and be amazing. She worked with fitness trainers to strengthen her muscles. She used resistance bands while she threw a heavy ball. Her legs burned, but she fought the pain.

Some coaches thought she was a diva. A diva is someone who thinks they are very important. But they realized Naomi was just very shy and reserved. She was always humble and polite to her coaches. At age fourteen, she became a pro player. She played tennis during the day and was homeschooled in the evenings.

Naomi's big breakthrough came in 2018 at the US Open. She beat her idol, Serena Williams, and won both sets. However, she was booed by the crowd who loved Serena. This was very hard on Naomi. In 2019, she won the Australian Open. But by 2021, right before the French Open, she made a decision. She announced that she would not do media interviews anymore. She felt they made her depression worse. She was fined $15,000 for refusing. The next day, she withdrew from the tournament to take care of her mental health.

She took a break from tennis. Naomi wanted time with her friends and family. She has shared some of the things that help her: therapy, her dog, calming music, and slowing down are some of them. Naomi says she's learned that you can never please everyone. The champion swimmer Michael Phelps also suffers from depression. He told her that by speaking up she may have saved a life. Naomi said, "If that's true, then it was all worth it."

As Naomi says, "It's OK to not be OK."

"You may lose more than you win . . . but if you put in the work, you can be the best version of yourself."

—Naomi Osaka

LOOK AT THE PAINTING When you look at the painting, you can see the message, "It's OK to not be OK." But there are other messages that are partly hidden on her shoulders if you look closely. One of them says, "In real life things aren't exactly the way you planned." What does that mean to you? Have you ever had a plan turn out differently than what you wanted?

its ok to not be ok
It's O.K. To Not Be O.K. It's O.K. To Not Be O.K. It's O.K.
Female Athlete of the Year 2020 won 4 Grand Slam tennis player for the Women's Association Female Athlete
Titles ranked as top tennis player for the Women's Association Female Athlete of the Year Grand Slam Titles ranked as
Tennis Association Female Athlete of the Year Grand Slam Titles ranked as

Malala Yousafzai
Fearless Advocate for Girls' Education

Born 1997 in Pakistan

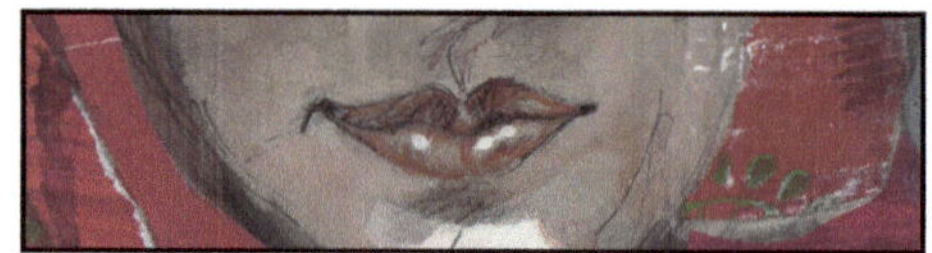

Malala's early childhood was happy and peaceful. Even though she lived in Pakistan, where girls were considered less than boys, she had a loving father. Unlike many girls in Pakistan, her father believed in education for all. Her father was a teacher and activist. An activist is someone who works to bring about change and make the world a better place. Her dad started a girls' high school, so girls would have the same opportunities as boys.

Like many kids, Malala loved TV. When she was young, she watched a TV show called *Shaka Laka Boom Boom*. In it, a boy named Sanji had a magic pencil. It could make anything real just by drawing it! When Sanji and his friends got in trouble, the magic pencil got them out of it. Malala wished for a magic pencil to draw a better world without poverty and war, where girls and boys could be equals.

When Malala was ten years old, the Taliban invaded their area. The Taliban were strict Muslims who brought in new laws. They destroyed or shut down schools and demanded that girls be banned from getting an education. Their laws said women had to stay home and only go out if they wore a burqa which covered them from head to toe. Girls were not allowed to be seen in public without a male relative. Women could no longer have jobs or vote. TV, movies, and dancing were banned or forbidden.

All Malala wanted was an education. But what could a young girl do? A LOT!! At eleven years old, she joined a protest against school closings. She gave a speech on TV titled, "How Dare the Taliban Take Away My Basic Right to Education." That speech became famous. She wrote blogs about life under the Taliban, using a different name for herself. When her identity was revealed, she started to speak in public. For a while, the ban was lifted, but war broke out in Pakistan, and Malala's family had to flee their area.

In 2011, she was awarded the International Children's Peace Prize, one of many honors. By then, she was getting death threats, but did that stop her? Absolutely not! She never gave up speaking out for girls' right to learn.

In 2012, at age fifteen, she was riding the school bus home. A Taliban gunman rushed onto the bus and shot her in the head. She survived and was flown to England for surgery. After an amazing recovery, Malala celebrated her sixteenth birthday by giving a speech at the United Nations. Millions of people around the world supported her cause and signed a petition. Finally, there was free education for all kids in Pakistan.

She was named one of *Time* magazine's Most Influential People at age sixteen. At seventeen, she received the Nobel Peace Prize. Though the Taliban tried to stop her, mighty Malala would not be pushed around by their bullying. **In her own words, "If one man can destroy everything, why can't one girl change it?"**

LOOK AT THE PAINTING Why do you think the artist painted the background like a chalkboard? Do you see the black symbols near Malala's face? What do you think they might be?

يوه نجلۍ هرڅه بدلولی شي
one girl can
n change

"One child, one teacher, one book,
one pen can change the world."
—Malala Yousafzai

X Gonzalez
Gun Control Activist

Born 1999 in Parkland, Florida

X Gonzalez is feisty and funny. They joke about giving their parents a PowerPoint slideshow to convince them to let them get a buzz cut. In it, they said things like "save money, spend less on shampoo." X said their dad laughed so hard at their presentation, but in the end, they were allowed to do it. People ask if their hair is a political statement. Their answer is "No, it's too hot in Florida, and it felt like wearing a sweater on my head."

X was born to Cuban parents, their father a lawyer and their mom a math teacher. They love cats, astronomy, and creative writing. They hate math. Like many teens, they love TV and movies. But as a student at Marjory Stoneman Douglas High School in Parkland, Florida, they survived a brutal mass shooting that killed seventeen of their classmates and teachers.

X was in a class in the auditorium when the alarms went off. Students were told to take cover between the seats, but they didn't know what was happening. X held their friend's hands to calm them down.

Three days later, X gave an amazing speech at a gun-control rally. The rally was on TV. They became famous for saying, "We call BS," after politicians said no laws could have prevented the shooting tragedy.

With fellow students and activists all over the country, they planned student walkouts to protest gun violence. X and other students founded the group Never Again MSD. They worked to get stricter gun-control policies and to encourage young people to vote.

At age eighteen, X gave a passionate speech at the March for Our Lives rally in Washington, DC. Small but mighty, they stood on boxes to reach the microphone. They listed the names of the students and staff who were gunned down at their school. During the speech there was a period of silence until six minutes and twenty seconds had passed. This was the amount of time it took the shooter to kill seventeen people and injure fifteen more. X gave a brave and powerful speech that any adult would have been proud of.

This tiny powerhouse never lost their cool and always held their own with the adults in power. President Barack Obama was so impressed that he wrote about them. It's no wonder that *Time* magazine named X "One of the 100 Most Influential People" in 2018.

During college, X came out as nonbinary and changed their name and their pronouns to they/them. They choose X to honor Malcolm X, a civil rights activist. X is proud that the work they did helped create 278 stricter gun laws throughout the country. **But their work is not done, and you can bet that X will shake things up!**

"They say no laws could have prevented the hundreds of senseless tragedies that have occurred. We call BS."

—X Gonzalez

 Why do you think X has their eyes closed and their hand on their head? What does "Never Again" mean to you?

NEVER
AGAIN

Greta Thunberg
Climate Crisis Activist

Born 2003 in Stockholm, Sweden

In August 2019, Greta Thunberg decided to skip school. But unlike other kids who skip school, she was not out for a good time. Instead, wearing a yellow raincoat, she hopped on her bike and rode to the Parliament House (the government building). She was armed with a wooden sign her dad helped her make that said (in Swedish of course!) School Strike for Climate. She also made one hundred flyers and posted about it on social media. Sadly, Greta stood alone the whole day until three. No one joined her. At barely five feet tall, fifteen-year-old Greta seemed to be on her own.

Greta did not give up. She contacted newspapers to tell them about her strike. She posted photos of her holding her sign on Instagram and Twitter. Finally, on day three, others joined her. Soon hundreds and thousands all over the world took part in the movement to save our climate.

When Greta and her sister Beata were young, their parents taught them good habits for our environment. They turned off lights when they left a room, did not waste water, and rode bikes instead of asking for rides in a car. Her parents even bought an electric car instead of using gas for fuel.

Greta's childhood was a loving one. She loved piano, ballet, horses, and especially her golden retriever, Moses, and rescue dog, Roxy. She loved to read and often seemed more like a grown-up than a child.

When Greta was eight, her class watched a film about global warming and the harm it is doing to our planet. She began worrying so much that by age eleven, she fell into a depression. She stopped eating, talking, and going to school. Her parents were so worried that they took her to a children's hospital. After many tests, doctors found Greta had Asperger's syndrome. It is a mild form of autism. That explained to Greta why she saw everything as either black or white, right or wrong. Though smart and talented, it helped her understand why social situations were hard for her.

In February 2018, Greta heard about the tragic mass killings of students in Parkland, Florida. The students at that high school organized anti-gun protests that inspired more protests around the world. Greta asked a friend, "What if children did that for the climate?"

After her first strike at the Parliament, she started her Fridays for Future campaign in September 2018. Students all over the world began their own strikes for climate change awareness. She spoke at the United Nations Climate Conference. She was interviewed on TV and named *Time* magazine's Person of the Year for 2019. She was nominated for the Nobel Peace Prize in 2019.

She was only sixteen years old!

But Greta didn't care about the fame or honors. She simply wanted people to DO SOMETHING. She said, "I want you to act as if your house is on fire. Because it is."

"The one thing we need more than hope is action. Once we start to act, hope is everywhere."

For all of you reading this, remember what Greta said. **"You are never too small to make a difference."**

"No one *is* too small to make a difference."

–Greta Thunberg

 Greta looks very serious in the painting with flames in the background and the words "Our house is on fire." She was small and young but wanted people to listen to her. Have you ever felt like you had something important to say, but no one would listen? If so, what did you do?

Our house is on fire.
"Act as you w...
ct as you would
in a crisis.
Our house is on fire
Once we start to act hope is everywhere. The o
more than hope is action. Once we start to act. Once
"The one thing we need more than hope is action.
hope is everywhere." The one thing we need more th
Once we start
re th

Bibliography

Duster, Michelle. *Ida B the Queen*. Simon & Schuster, 2021

Duster, Michelle. *Ida B Wells*. *Voice of Truth*. Godwin Books, 2022

Myers, Walter Dean. *Ida B Wells: Let the Truth Be Told*. Amazon, 2008

Gillibrand, Kirsten. *Bold and Brave Ten Heroes Who Won Women the Right to Vote*. Random House, 2018

Kennedy, Nancy B. *Women Win the Vote*. Norton Young Readers, 2020

Adams, Katherine H., and Michael L. Keene. *Alice Paul and the American Woman Suffrage Campaign*. Chicago: University of Illinois Press, 2008.

Alexander, Kerri Lee. *RBG*. National Women's History Museum, 2020

Donvito, Tina. "15 Ways Justice Ruth Bader Ginsburg Has Made History," *Reader's Digest*, 2023.

Franke, Katherine, The Center for Gender and Sexual Equality. Columbia University, 2020.

Rosen, Jeffrey. "RBG's Life in Her Own Words." *The Atlantic*, 2020.

Lewis, Aura. *Gloria's Voice*. *Sterling Juvenile*, 2018.

McLaughlin, Katie. *Five Things Women Couldn't Do in the Sixties*. CNN, 2014.

Fabiny, Sarah. *Who is Gloria Steinem?* Penguin Random House, 2014.

Michaels, Debra. *Gloria Steinem*. National Women's History Museum, 2017.

Vegara, Maria Isabel Sanchez. *Little People Big Dreams*. Amazon, 2020.

Russel-Brown, Katheryn. *A Voice Named Aretha*. Bloomsbury Children's Books, 2020.

Pareles, Jon. "Aretha Franklin." *New York Times*, 2018.

Miller, Julie. "Aretha Franklin Interview." *Vanity Fair*, 2021.

Aretha Franklin. "PBS NewsHour", 2019.

Twen, Rachel. *Edie Windsor*. Jewish Women's Archive, 2021.

Socredo, Richard. "The Legacy of Edie Windsor." *The New Yorker*, 2017.

Gray, Eliza. "Edie Windsor, The Unlikely Activist." *Time* magazine, 2013.

Windsor, Edie, Lyon, Joshua. *A Wild and Precious Life*. St Martin's Publishing Group, 2021.

Chavez, Nicole and Saeed Ahmed. "What We Know About Emma Gonzalez." CNN, 2018

"Call Me 'X.'" Interview. *The Tonight Show with Jimmy Fallon*, 2021.

Gonzalez, X. "The Education of X." *The Cut*, 2023.

Eller, Claudia. "Emma Gonzalez Opens Up." *Variety Magazine*, 2018.

Yousafzai, Malala and Lamb, Christine. *I Am Malala*. Little Brown & Co., 2013.

"Girls Can! Smash Stereotypes, Defy Expectations and Make History." *National Geographic Kids*, 2020.

Yousafzai, Malala. *Malala's Magic Pencil*. Little Brown & Co., 2017.

Malala Fund, 2022.

Harken, Amy. *Rosa Parks Biography for Kids*. Lottie.com, 2015.

Woodward, Kay. *What Would She Do?*. Carlton Books, 2018.

Harrison, Vashti. *Little Leaders—Bold Women in Black History*. Little, Brown Books for Young Readers, 2017.

Rosa Parks In Her Own Words. Library of Congress, 2022.

Collection: Rosa Parks Papers. Library of Congress, 2016.

Brownridge, Lucy. *Portrait of An Artist Frida Kahlo*. Quarto Publishers, 2019.

Fabiny, Sarah. *Who Was Frida Kahlo?*. Grosset & Dunlap, 2013.

Tuchman, Phyllis. "Frida Kahlo." *Smithsonian Magazine*, November 2002.

"Lozen: The Fearless Apache Warrior Woman You've Probably Never Heard Of." Kumeyaay.com

Life Story: Lozen (ca 1840-1889). Women and the American Story. New York Historical Society

Tekaroniake Evans, Tony. *The Apache Woman Warrior Who Helped Lead Resistance to European Invaders.* History Channel, July 2023.

Lorde, Audre. *Sister Outsider.* Crossing Press, 2007.

Lorde, Audre. *The Cancer Journals.* Penguin Classics, 2020.

DeVeaux, Alexis. *Warrior Poet A Biography of Audre Lorde.* W. W. Norton & Company, 2006.

Harkin, Sofia. *Emmeline Pankhurst Biography for Kids.* Lottie.com, 2015.

Emmeline Pankhurst. Iowa State University Archives of Women's Political Communication, 1995-2023.

Capaldi, Gina. *Red Bird Sings—The Story of Zitkala-Sa.* Carolrhoda Books, 2019.

"Zitkala-Sa: Trailblazing American Composer." *Unladylike 2020 American Masters,* PBS.

Life Story: Zitkala-Sa, aka Gertrude Simmons Bonnin (1876-1938). Women & The American Story. nyhistory.org

LeClair, Mary K., Justin D. White, and Susan Keeter. *Three 19th Century Women Doctors.* Hofmann Press, 2007.

Staten, Candace. *Sarah Loguen Fraser (1850-1933).* BlackPast.org, 2014.

Gupta, Boshika. "*The Untold Truth of Naomi Osaka*" "Grunge", 2021.

Fishman, Jon. *Sports All-Stars Naomi Osaka.* Lerner Publications, 2021.

Rothberg, Emma. *Naomi Osaka.* National Women's History Museum, 2022.

Simone Biles. Kidskonnect.com, 2021.

"This is Simone: Read the Story of Simone Biles." *Time for Kids,* 2020.

McDaniels, Andrea K. "Simone Biles and the Power of a Woman's Voice." *Baltimore Sun,* 2021.

Correa, Carla. "How many Olympic medals does Biles have?." *New York Times,* 2021.

Mosca, Julia Finley. *The Girl Who Thought in Pictures: The story of Dr. Temple Grandin.* The Innovation Press, 2019.

DeMuth, Patricia Brennan. *Who Is Temple Grandin?* Penguin Workshop, 2020.

Montgomery, Sy. *Temple Grandin: How the Girl Who Loved Cows Embraced Autism and Changed the World.* Clarion Books, 2014.

The World Needs All Kinds of Minds. PBS, 2014.

Guglielmo, Amy. *How to Build a Hug: Temple Grandin and Her Amazing Squeeze Machine.* Atheneum Books for Young Readers, 2018.

Leonard, Jill. *Who is Greta Thunberg?* Penguin, 2020.

Thunberg, Greta. *No One is Too Small to Make a Difference.* Penguin, 2018.

Deeded, Matt. *Greta Thunberg Climate Crisis Activist.* Lerner Publishing, 2021.

"Greta Thunberg Facts." *National Geographic for Kids,* 2020.

Keefe, Anna. *5 Greta Thunberg-Inspired Ways to Be an Environmentalist.* T. Colin Campbell Center for Nutrition Studies, 2021.

"Women in Innovation—Interview With Dr. Ochoa." United States Patent & Trademark Office, 2018.

Mosca, Julia Finley. *The Astronaut with a Song for the Stars: The Story of Dr. Ellen Ochoa.* The Innovation Press, 2019.

Jaffe, Elizabeth D. *Ellen Ochoa.* Children's Press, 2005

Ochoa, Ellen. *Dr. Ochoa's Stellar World: We Are All Scientists / Todos solos científicos.* Lil' Libros, 2022

Rappaport, Doreen. *Ellen Takes Flight: The Life of Astronaut Ellen Ochoa.* Little, Brown Books for Young Readers, 2023

Who Inspires You?

I have invited some of my former students
to choose a strong woman who inspires
them and do a portrait of her. Here are
some of their creations.

Rosa Parks by Judith age 8

Simone Biles by Nora age 11

Melanie Martinez by Isla age 12

About Atmosphere Press

Founded in 2015, Atmosphere Press was built on the principles of Honesty, Transparency, Professionalism, Kindness, and Making Your Book Awesome. As an ethical and author-friendly hybrid press, we stay true to that founding mission today.

If you're a reader, enter our giveaway for a free book here:

SCAN TO ENTER
BOOK GIVEAWAY

If you're a writer, submit your manuscript for consideration here:

SCAN TO SUBMIT
MANUSCRIPT

And always feel free to visit Atmosphere Press and our authors online at atmospherepress.com. See you there soon!

About the Author

PAULA KERMAN grew up in Kansas City, Missouri, but has made Des Moines, Iowa, her home since attending college at Drake University, where she completed a bachelor of fine arts degree. She also has a master's in education and was an art educator for forty-three years in the Des Moines Public Schools, at the Des Moines Art Center, and at her in-home studio. She is passionate about her art practice and has exhibited and sold her work. After experiencing significant loss, she began researching and painting strong women who inspired her. *Hooligans, Rebels, and Rabble-Rousers* is her first book.